Resilient Calm

Confident

Riding the Waves of Life

H.M. Mann

Inner Radiance Publishing

Contents

About The Author H. M. Mann

Dedicated to all hearts searching for calm, peace, and clarity.
This book is for the young and the young at heart,
as well as for anyone open to a fresh perspective.

Introduction

Resilient Calm Confident: Riding the Waves of Life

Welcome to the Journey.

Thank you for choosing this guide. Whether you're here because you've had a challenging day, you're seeking tools to navigate life's ups and downs, or you're simply curious about what this book has to offer, I'm truly glad you're here.

By opening these pages, you've already taken a meaningful step toward finding balance and understanding in your life, and that can give you courage, hope and enthusiasm.

It's likely that you've found yourself in a moment where your feelings seem overwhelming, your mind feels like it's spiraling, or your body feels out of sync. Whether it's because of stress, hormones, sadness, or just life being unpredictable, you're not alone. We all face tough days, but it doesn't have to mean we're lost or broken.

Why This Guide?

This guide is here to help you take care of yourself during those days when everything feels a little heavy. It's filled with simple, powerful tools and affirmations to remind you that even in the toughest times, you have the strength to come through it. And most importantly, it will encourage you to approach yourself and the world around you with kindness, compassion, and a broad sense of connection to the universe. Let's be honest: life can be unpredictable.

One moment, everything feels fine, and the next, it's as if the world has turned upside down. Maybe you're dealing with pressure at school or work, challenges in relationships, or simply the weight of figuring out who you are and where you fit in the world. It can feel like you're caught in a storm with no clear way out. But here's the thing about storms, they don't last forever. And even when the waves are rough, you have the strength to ride through them.

This book is here to be your companion during those moments when everything feels a little too heavy.

Think of it as a toolkit, filled with simple, powerful strategies to help you:

Understand your emotions so they don't feel so overwhelming.

Build self-compassion so you can treat yourself with kindness instead of judgment.

Learn to find calm through mindful breathing and grounding techniques.

Feel connected to something bigger than yourself, reminding you that you're never truly alone.

This is about giving you new skills, an inner connection to confidence and a sense of purpose. It's about helping you see the strength, resilience, and beauty that already exist within you.

A Word About Tough Days

Tough days happen to everyone. You might feel overwhelmed by sadness, frustration, or fear. Your mind might race with negative thoughts, or your body might feel heavy and tired. You might even think, "Why is this happening to me?" It's okay to feel this way.

Emotions are a natural part of being human, and while they can be intense, they are temporary. Just like waves in the ocean, they rise, peak, and eventually fade. This book will help you navigate those waves with a sense of calm and confidence.

What You'll Find in This Book

Each chapter is designed to help you face life's challenges with greater ease. You'll learn:

How to understand and accept your feelings without letting them take over.

How to be kind to yourself, even when you feel like you've messed up.

Practical exercises like mindful breathing and grounding to help you find balance.

How to connect to the bigger picture and trust your journey.

Throughout the book, you'll also find affirmations, short, powerful statements you can repeat to yourself to build strength and hope. These affirmations are like mental anchors, helping you stay steady when the waves feel rough.

In an ever-evolving world, where change is the only constant, it's entirely natural to experience a profound sense of uncertainty. Our lives are marked by distinct seasons of change, each laden with its own set of challenges that can trigger feelings of anxiety, stress, and worry.

My deepest hope is that this guide becomes a beacon of support, offering you a safe haven, and arming you with practical tools to navigate the complex journey of life.

We all yearn to carve out lives filled with fulfillment, deep connections, meaningful experiences, and a strong sense of purpose. Yet, the inevitable encounters with change, loss, crisis, or unforeseen challenges can shake our foundational sense of security to its core.

In these moments, the importance of having a well-established personal framework, comprising self-support, compassion, and a set of practical skills, becomes undeniably crucial. This framework acts as our anchor, enabling us to navigate through life's tumultuous waters with grace and resilience.

This book is for everyone, teens, young adults, and adults alike. Whether you're just starting your journey or have been walking this path for some time, the content is tailored to meet your needs.

Each section offers insights and tools relevant to different life stages and challenges. What makes this guide unique are its practical exercises and real-life stories. These elements make the strategies accessible and applicable to your personal and professional life. You will find tools that you can use to enhance your emotional intelligence and resilience.

As you begin this journey, I want to assure you that you are not alone. This book will provide tangible tools and insights to help you build emotional resilience and improve your quality of life. You will find guidance and support along the way.

I invite you to actively engage with the exercises and reflections throughout the book. Personal involvement is key to developing emotional resilience. These activities are designed to help you connect with your inner strength and find your unique path to well-being.

A Personal Note

Allow me to introduce myself. I am H. M. Mann, a counselor and therapist with 27 plus years of experience working in a variety of settings (hospitals, recovery centers, and outpatient clinics). I have had the privilege of helping people from diverse backgrounds and cultures. My work has focused on emotional resilience, healing, and personal growth. I believe in the power of compassion, warmth, and creative problem-solving.

I want you to know that you're not alone in this. Everyone, no matter how confident they seem, goes through tough days. The important thing is to remember that you have the tools to get through them. Even when the storm feels endless, there's always calm on the other side. So take a deep breath, open your heart, and let's begin this journey together. The waves may come, but you are stronger than you know. Together, we'll learn how to ride them. Welcome to the beginning of something powerful: the discovery of your own inner strength. Let's dive in.

Affirmation to Start the Journey:

"I am ready to face life's waves with courage, compassion, and hope. I have everything I need within me to find balance and peace."

Understanding the Storms

♥

Chapter 1: Understanding the Storms

Life can feel like a rollercoaster, with emotions and experiences coming at you faster than you can process them. One minute, everything feels fine, and the next, you're caught in a whirlwind of sadness, frustration, or anxiety. These "storms" are part of being human, but when they happen, it's easy to feel overwhelmed and wonder if something is wrong with you. The truth is, these emotional ups and downs are often a natural response to what's happening in your mind, body, and environment.

Stress at work or school, changes in friendships, pressure to succeed, or even chemistry imbalances in the body can stir up intense feelings that seem impossible to manage. But the good news? Feelings, like storms, are temporary. They might feel all-consuming in the moment, but they always pass. When the world around us appears to be shifting and changing under our very feet, this may elicit a deeply unsettled feeling of uncertainty. We each face multiple seasons of change throughout our lives which bring with them many triggers for anxiety, stress and worry. If you have found your way to this work, it is my sincere hope that you will find a safe haven of support, understanding, and useful tools to aid in your life journey.

Understandably, each of us seeks to create a life path that builds fulfillment and connection, meaning and purpose. When change, loss, crisis, or the unexpected occurs, our very sense of having a stable reference point for security can be shaken to the core. In these moments, we need to have already built a bridge towards self supportive, compassionate, and useful perspectives, behaviors and skills that will carry us across the rough waters of life.

What Are the Storms?

Sometimes, it's hard to explain why you feel the way you do. It can feel like your body is acting on its own, your emotions are all over the place, or your thoughts are racing and spinning. This is often the result of things like hormonal changes, stress, or external pressures, and it's completely normal. Your feelings and emotions, however intense, don't define you. They are temporary. Like the weather, they come and go, and your job is simply to ride the waves and know they will pass.

Why Do Emotional Storms Happen?

Understanding why emotions can feel so intense is the first step toward riding them out. Here's what's going on beneath the surface:

Your Brain is Ever Changing and Adapting

Your brain, especially the parts responsible for regulating emotions and making decisions, is under construction until we are at least 25. This means it's completely normal to feel like your emotions sometimes take over before your logical brain can step in.

Stress and Hormonal Changes

As your body goes through different stages of life, periods of stress, and changes in lifestyle, hormonal and body chemistry shifts can affect your mental and emotional state.

Affirmation for the Day:

"I am more than my feelings today. I am a whole being, capable of riding through this storm with compassion and care."

Navigating Uncertainty with Confidence

Life is a journey filled with twists, turns, and unexpected detours. For young adults, the uncertainty of what lies ahead can often feel overwhelming. From academic pressures to social challenges, personal goals, and even global events, navigating the unknown can sometimes stir up feelings of anxiety and self-doubt. This chapter is your guide to embracing uncertainty with confidence, equipping you with tools to face challenges with resilience and a sense of hope.

Understanding Uncertainty and Why It Feels Difficult

Uncertainty is a natural part of life, yet it can be uncomfortable because our brains are wired to seek patterns and predict outcomes. When faced with the unknown, it's normal to feel anxious or uneasy. Acknowledging these feelings is the first step to managing them. It's okay to not have all the answers right away, what matters is how you respond to the uncertainty.

Quick Reflection: Think about a time when you faced an uncertain situation. How did you feel? What helped you get through it?

Building Your Inner Toolkit

Developing tools to navigate uncertainty can help you feel more grounded and prepared. Here are some strategies to cultivate:

Practice Mindfulness: Stay present in the moment. Focusing on what you can control right now can reduce feelings of overwhelm. Try this: Sit quietly, take a deep breath, and name five things you can see, four things you can touch, three things you can hear, two things you can smell, and one thing you can taste. This practice helps anchor you in the present.

Cultivate Gratitude:
Shifting your focus to what you're grateful for can foster a sense of stability and positivity. Consider keeping a gratitude journal where you write down three things you're thankful for each day. Set Small, Achievable Goals: Break big tasks or challenges into smaller, manageable steps. Celebrate your progress, no matter how small.

The Power of Perspective

When faced with uncertainty, your perspective can shape your experience. Instead of seeing the unknown as a threat, try to view it as an opportunity for growth and discovery. Challenges often lead to new insights, skills, and strengths you never knew you had. Exercise: Reflect on a past challenge that seemed daunting at first. What did you learn or gain from the experience? How did it help you grow?

Building a Support System

You don't have to navigate uncertainty alone. Surround yourself with supportive friends, family, mentors, or trusted adults who can provide guidance and encouragement. Sharing your thoughts and feelings can lighten the emotional load. Action Step: Identify three people in your life you can turn to for support during uncertain times. Consider how you might reach out to them when you need help.

Embracing Self-Compassion

Be kind to yourself as you navigate uncertain times. It's normal to make mistakes or feel unsure. Treat yourself with the same compassion and understanding you would offer a friend. Self-Compassion Exercise: Write a letter to yourself as if you were comforting a friend in the same situation. What words of encouragement and support would you offer?

Reframing Fear

Fear often accompanies uncertainty, but it doesn't have to hold you back. Instead of avoiding fear, try reframing it as a sign that you're stepping out of your comfort zone and into a space of growth.

Affirmation: Repeat this to yourself: "I am capable of handling whatever comes my way. Each step I take brings me closer to my goals."

Practicing Flexibility and Adaptability

Uncertainty requires flexibility, the ability to adjust and adapt to changing circumstances. Practice being open to new ideas, approaches, and solutions.

Challenge: Try something new this week that takes you slightly out of your comfort zone. It could be trying a new hobby, talking to someone new, or exploring a different perspective on a familiar issue.

Finding Meaning in the Unknown

Uncertain times can be opportunities to discover what truly matters to you. Reflect on your values, passions, and goals. Use the unknown as a chance to align your actions with what feels meaningful and fulfilling. Journal Prompt: What do I value most in life? How can I stay true to these values, even during uncertain times?

Staying Grounded

When life feels overwhelming, grounding techniques can help you feel more centered and in control. Grounding Exercise: Take slow, deep breaths. Place your feet firmly on the ground. Focus on the sensations of your body and the space around you. Remind yourself: "In this moment, I am safe."

Celebrating Progress

Every step you take toward embracing uncertainty is a victory. Celebrate your resilience and courage, no matter how small your accomplishments may seem. Reflection Activity: Create a list of three things you're proud of today.

Acknowledge your efforts and growth.

H.M. MANN

Uncertainty is an inevitable part of life, but it doesn't have to define your experience. By cultivating resilience, embracing self-compassion, and leaning on your support system, you can navigate even the most challenging times with confidence. Remember, you have the strength within you to face the unknown and emerge stronger, wiser, and more empowered than ever.

Chapter 2:
Self-Compassion:
Being Your Own
Best Friend

♥

When the world feels heavy, it's easy to be hard on yourself. You might feel like you should be "better" or that something's wrong with you. But the truth is, you're allowed to have days when you don't feel okay. You don't need to be perfect. Start by treating yourself like you would treat a friend who is struggling. If your friend was sad, would you tell them to "snap out of it" or would you listen to them, offer kindness, and encourage them to be gentle with themselves?

What is Self-Compassion?

Self-compassion is about treating yourself with the same kindness, understanding, and care you would offer to a good friend. It's recognizing that you're human, which means you're allowed to have bad days, make mistakes, and feel a range of emotions without judging yourself harshly. Too often, we're our own worst critics. When things go wrong, we might think, "I'm such a failure" or "Why can't I be better at this?" But imagine saying those things to a friend who's struggling. You wouldn't, right? You'd likely encourage them and remind them of their worth. Self-compassion is about turning that same kindness inward.

Why is Self-Compassion Important?

When you're hard on yourself, it can make tough times feel even heavier. Instead of helping you improve, self-criticism can create feelings of shame, guilt, and self-doubt.

On the other hand, self-compassion can:

- Help you bounce back from setbacks.
- Reduce feelings of stress and anxiety.
- Build resilience and emotional strength.
- Teach you that you're worthy of love and care.

Self-compassion doesn't mean ignoring mistakes or giving up on growth. Instead, it's about accepting where you are right now and supporting yourself as you move forward.

How to Practice Self-Compassion

Speak to Yourself Kindly

Notice the words you use when you talk to yourself. Are they supportive or critical? When you catch yourself being harsh, pause and ask, "What would I say to a friend in this situation?" Then, speak those words to yourself. For example: Instead of: "I'm so stupid for failing that test." Try: "That test was tough, but I did my best. I'll learn from this and try again."

Acknowledge Your Feelings Without Judgment

It's okay to feel sad, frustrated, or angry. Instead of pushing those feelings away, try naming them. For example, say, "I'm feeling really disappointed right now, and that's okay." This simple act of acknowledgment can help you process your emotions without getting stuck in them.

Take a Self-Compassion Break

When you're feeling overwhelmed, try this practice: Pause and take a deep breath. Place a hand on your heart or give yourself a gentle hug. Say to yourself: "This is a tough moment. It's okay to feel this way. I am here for myself, and I am doing my best."

Practice Self-Care Without Guilt

Taking care of yourself is not selfish, it's essential. Whether it's taking a nap, enjoying your favorite hobby, or just spending time alone, self-care is a way to recharge and show yourself love. Remind yourself that you deserve rest and kindness.

Self-Compassion in Action:

A Story

Imagine you had a rough day at work or school. You forgot your project or homework, argued with a coworker or friend, and felt out of place during lunch. When you get home, the first thing you want to do is replay all your mistakes and tell yourself you're a failure. Instead, what if you paused and treated yourself like a friend? You might say, "Today was hard, but it doesn't define who I am. I'm learning and growing, and it's okay to have off days. Tomorrow is a new chance to try again." This shift in perspective allows you to move forward without the weight of self-judgment.

Self-compassion isn't something you master overnight, it's a practice. The more you make space for it, the easier it becomes to treat yourself with kindness, even on tough days.

Affirmation and Reflection
Daily Affirmation: "I am worthy of love and kindness, even when I feel like I'm struggling. I will treat myself with the same care I offer to others."

Questions for Reflection:
What's one kind thing I can say to myself today?
How would I support a friend going through the same feelings I'm having right now?
What's one small way I can be supportive of myself today?

Self-compassion is about learning to be your own safe place, it isn't about fixing yourself. On tough days, remind yourself that it's okay to feel however you feel and that you're doing the best you can. Keep practicing, and over time, self-compassion will become your natural response to life's challenges.

Self-Compassion Practice:

When you're feeling down, place a hand on your heart and say, "It's okay to feel this way. I am worthy of love, care, and space, just as I am." Let that be your reminder that you don't need to fix yourself, just take good loving care of yourself.

Chapter 3:
Breathing Through
the Waves

♥

Why Breathing Matters

When your emotions are running high, your body can feel out of control. But one of the simplest ways to bring calm back is to focus on your breath. It's a tool you always have with you, and it's a great way to reset your mind and body. When emotions feel overwhelming, it's easy to lose control, your heart races, your chest tightens, and your thoughts spiral. This is your body's natural "fight or flight" response, designed to protect you in moments of danger. But when there's no immediate threat (just strong emotions or stress), this response can make everything feel worse. Breathing is one of the most powerful tools you have to calm your body and mind. It's always with you, it's free, and it only takes a few moments to shift your focus. By learning how to breathe intentionally, you can create a sense of calm, even in the middle of a storm.

Breathing Exercise: Square Breathing

Find a quiet space where you can sit comfort ably. If you can, close your eyes. Breathe in deeply through your nose for 4 seconds, filling your belly with air. Hold your breath gently for 4 seconds. Exhale slowly and completely for 4 seconds, releasing any tension. Hold your breath gently for 4 seconds.Repeat this for 3-5 minutes, focusing only on the rise and fall of your breath. As you breathe, imagine each breath is filling you with vital life force energy, light and peace, transforming the storm within you into a calm lake.

What Happens When You Breathe?

Deep, intentional breathing does more than just bring air into your lungs, it sends signals to your brain and body to relax. When you breathe deeply: Your heart rate slows down. Your muscles release tension. Your mind becomes clearer, allowing you to think more calmly. Stress hormones (like cortisol) decrease, helping you feel more balanced. It's like hitting the reset button for your body and emotions.

The Calm Wave Breathing Exercise

This simple exercise can help you reset when you're feeling over-whelmed. It's called "The Calm Wave" because each breath is like a wave in the ocean, flowing in and out, soothing and steady.

Find a Quiet Space: Sit or lie down comfortably. If you can, close your eyes to limit distractions. Inhale Slowly: Breathe deeply through your nose for 4 seconds, letting the air fill your belly like a balloon. Hold Your Breath: Gently hold your breath for 7 seconds, allowing the air to settle within you.   Exhale Fully: Breathe out slowly and completely through your mouth for 8 seconds. Imagine releasing all your tension with the breath. Repeat: Continue this cycle for 5 to 10 minutes and notice the profound change that you feel physically and emotionally.

Alternate Nostril Breathing: A Pathway to Calm and Balance

Alternate nostril breathing, also known as *Nadi Shodhana* in San-skrit, is a powerful yet simple technique that can bring calm, clarity, and balance to your mind and body. This ancient practice, rooted in yogic traditions, helps regulate the flow of breath and energy channels within the body. Whether you're looking to manage stress, center yourself, or simply cultivate a deeper sense of inner peace, alternate nostril breathing is a tool you can turn to anytime, anywhere.

At its core, alternate nostril breathing works by alternating the inhale and exhale between the left and right nostrils. This creates a rhythmic and balanced breathing pattern that promotes relaxation and enhances mental focus. By engaging in this practice regularly, you can calm the nervous system, reduce anxiety, and restore a sense of harmony within yourself.

Preparing for the Practice

Before beginning, find a quiet and comfortable space where you won't be disturbed. Sit in a comfortable position, either on the floor with your legs crossed or on a chair with your feet firmly planted on the ground. Rest your hands on your knees or in your lap, and ensure that your spine is straight to allow for smooth and unrestricted breathing. If it helps, close your eyes to eliminate distractions and bring your focus inward.

Take a moment to ground yourself. Breathe naturally and observe your breath as it flows in and out. This brief moment of mindfulness sets the tone for your practice and prepares your body and mind for the experience ahead.

The Steps of Alternate Nostril Breathing

Position Your Hand: Using your dominant hand, bring your thumb and ring finger toward your nostrils. The thumb will be used to close the right nostril, and the ring finger will close the left nostril. Rest your index and middle fingers gently on your forehead or curl them inward.

Close the Right Nostril and Inhale: Gently press your thumb against your right nostril to close it. Inhale slowly and deeply through your left nostril, filling your lungs completely. Focus on the sensation of the breath as it enters your body.

Close the Left Nostril and Exhale: Use your ring finger to close your left nostril, releasing the thumb from your right nostril. Exhale slowly and fully through your right nostril. Empty your lungs completely, allowing your body to relax with the exhale.

Inhale Through the Right Nostril: With the left nostril still closed, inhale deeply and steadily through your right nostril. Feel the air filling your lungs.

Close the Right Nostril and Exhale Through the Left: Close your right nostril again with your thumb, releasing your ring finger from the left nostril. Exhale slowly and fully through your left nostril.

This completes one cycle of alternate nostril breathing. Continue this pattern for several minutes, maintaining a steady and relaxed rhythm. Aim for at least five to ten cycles to experience the full benefits.

Benefits of Alternate Nostril Breathing
Alternate nostril breathing offers a wide range of physical, mental, and emotional benefits.

Here are just a few: Calms the Nervous System: By slowing down your breath and focusing on the rhythm, this practice activates the parasympathetic nervous system, promoting relaxation and reducing stress. Improves Mental Clarity: The balanced breathing pattern helps clear mental fog, enhance concentration, and improve focus. Balances Energy: In yogic philosophy, the left nostril is associated with calming energy, while the right nostril represents energizing energy. Alternate nostril breathing harmonizes these energies, creating a sense of equilibrium. Reduces Anxiety: The deliberate and controlled breathing soothes the mind, making it an effective tool for managing anxiety and emotional overwhelm. Enhances Lung Capacity: Regular practice strengthens the lungs and improves overall respiratory function.

Tips for a Successful Practice

Go at Your Own Pace: There's no need to rush. Allow your breath to flow naturally and comfortably, adjusting the pace to suit your needs. Practice Regularly: To experience lasting benefits, incorporate alternate nostril breathing into your daily routine. Even five minutes a day can make a difference. Stay Patient: If your mind wanders during the practice, gently guide your focus back to your breath. Over time, this process becomes easier.

Listen to Your Body: If you ever feel lightheaded or uncomfortable, stop the practice and return to your natural breath. It's important to honor your body's signals.

Incorporating Alternate Nostril Breathing Into Your Life

Alternate nostril breathing can be practiced at any time of day. Use it in the morning to set a calm and focused tone for the day, during a stressful moment to find balance, or before bed to prepare for restful sleep. This versatile practice is your companion for navigating life's challenges with grace and composure. As you make alternate nostril breathing a part of your routine, you'll likely notice its transformative effects on your overall well-being. Each breath becomes an opportunity to reconnect with yourself, fostering a sense of calm and inner strength. Remember, the breath is always with you, a constant and grounding presence to guide you through life's ups and downs.

Affirmation to Pair with Breathing:

"With every breath, I return to my center. I am calm. I am here. I am safe."

Chapter 4:
The Heart of Mindfulness

♥

The True Meaning of Mindfulness: Heart Fullness

Mindfulness is a term that has become widely popular in recent years, but its origins hold a depth and richness that often go unnoticed. In the original Pali language, from which many foundational Buddhist texts are derived, the word that is often translated as "mindfulness" is "sati." However, a closer examination of the cultural and spiritual contexts reveals that "sati" might be more accurately understood as "heartfulness." This subtle yet profound distinction invites us to expand our understanding of mindfulness beyond the cognitive realm and into the domain of the heart.

The initial translation of "sati" into "mindfulness" occurred when European scholars first encountered Buddhist teachings in Southeast Asia. These academics, steeped in Western philosophies that prioritized reason and intellect, interpreted the term through a lens that emphasized mental processes. As a result, mindfulness came to be associated primarily with paying attention, observing thoughts, and cultivating present-moment awareness. While these aspects are indeed valuable, they represent only a portion of what "sati" encompasses.

In many Asian cultures, particularly among Indonesian and Balinese monks and spiritual practitioners, "sati" is understood as a quality that integrates both the mind and the heart. It embodies a sense of warmth, compassion, and connection that arises when we bring our full presence to the moment. In this sense, mindfulness is not just about observing life; it is about deeply feeling and engaging with it. It is an invitation to approach ourselves and others with kindness, curiosity, and a genuine sense of care.

The mistranslation of "sati" as "mindfulness" rather than "heartfulness" may reflect broader cultural differences in how emotions and relationships are valued. In Western traditions, there has historically been a tendency to separate the intellect from the emotions, viewing the mind as superior to the heart. By contrast, many Eastern philosophies see the mind and heart as inseparable, emphasizing the importance of cultivating both cognitive clarity and emotional depth.

This understanding of mindfulness as heartfulness can profoundly impact how we approach the practice. Rather than striving to quiet the mind or control our thoughts, we can focus on opening our hearts to whatever arises. Whether we are experiencing joy, sorrow, frustration, or fear, heartfulness encourages us to meet these emotions with acceptance and compassion. It is about creating a space within ourselves where all feelings are welcomed and honored.

Practicing heartfulness can also transform our relationships. When we approach others with a mindful heart, we listen more deeply, speak more authentically, and connect more fully. Heartfulness invites us to move beyond judgment and into empathy, recognizing the shared humanity that unites us all. It reminds us that mindfulness is not just an individual practice but a relational one, fostering greater under-standing and harmony in our interactions.

One way to cultivate heartfulness is through loving-kindness med-itation, a practice that involves silently repeating phrases of goodwill toward ourselves and others. For example, you might say, "May I be happy. May I be healthy. May I be safe. May I live with ease." Grad-ually, you extend these wishes to loved ones, acquaintances, and even those with whom you have conflicts. This practice helps to soften the boundaries between "self" and "other," nurturing a sense of intercon-nectedness and compassion.

Heartfulness can also be woven into everyday activities. Whether you are washing dishes, walking in nature, or sharing a meal with a friend, bring your attention to the sensations, emotions, and connec-tions present in the moment. Allow yourself to savor the experience fully, letting your heart guide your awareness. Over time, these small acts of heartfulness can create a profound shift in how you experience life.

As we reclaim the original meaning of mindfulness as heartfulness, we are reminded that this practice is not about perfection or achieving a particular state of mind. It is about showing up, again and again, with an open heart and a willingness to be present with whatever life brings. By embracing this deeper understanding, we can move beyond the limitations of the intellect and into the boundless wisdom of the heart, finding greater peace, connection, and joy along the way.

Heartfulness & Mindfulness in Action

When you're feeling sad or anxious, it's easy to get stuck in your thoughts. You might worry about the future, regret the past, or feel like things will never change. But the truth is, all you really have is this present moment. And in this moment, you have everything you need to start finding balance again.

Mindfulness (in it's original translation meant heart fullness) is simply noticing what's happening around you and inside of you with kindness and without judgment. It's like being a curious and compassionate scientist observing your thoughts and feelings with curiosity, instead of getting lost in them.

Mindfulness is the practice of being fully present in the moment, without judgment or distraction. It's about noticing what's happening around you and within you, your thoughts, feelings, and sensations, without trying to fix or change anything. Think of it as pressing "pause" on the whirlwind of life to simply be. When you're feeling stressed, anxious, or sad, your mind often races to the past ("Why did that happen?") or the future ("What if this goes wrong?"). Mindfulness helps you bring your attention back to the present moment, where your power to act and feel grounded resides.

Heartfulness & Mindfulness Practice:

The Grounding Technique

Take a deep breath and bring your attention to your feet. Wiggle your toes and notice the ground beneath you.

Slowly move your attention upward, notice how your body feels, the air around you, the sounds in the room.

Gently bring your attention to your body: What am I feeling in my body right now? Notice how your heart center feels?

Gently notice your thoughts: What am I thinking right now? Without trying to change them, just notice them.

Repeat the word "Here." with each breath, anchoring yourself in the present.

Gently place your hands over your heart: Breathe into your heart center while repeating "I accept myself and all of my feelings right now".

Why Mindfulness Matters

Life can be noisy, work, school, social media, family, and friends all demand your attention. When your mind gets pulled in too many directions, it's easy to feel over-

whelmed or disconnected. Mindfulness is like a mental reset button that helps you:

Calm racing thoughts and reduce anxiety.

Improve focus and decision-making.

Build emotional awareness and resilience.

Feel more connected to yourself and your surroundings.

Mindfulness doesn't mean you'll never feel stressed or upset again, it just gives you the tools to respond to those feelings with clarity and strength.

How to Practice Mindfulness

Start Small. You don't have to sit cross-legged on a mountaintop to practice mindfulness. It's something you can do anywhere, at any time, in small, simple ways. Even a few minutes of mindful breathing or observation can make a difference. Use Your Senses Your five senses are powerful anchors to the present moment. When you focus on what you can see, hear, feel, smell, or taste, your mind naturally slows down and tunes into the here and now.

Notice Without Judging

Mindfulness is about observing your thoughts and feelings, not fighting them. If you notice your mind wandering or feel uncomfortable emotions, don't criticize yourself. Simply say, "This is what I'm feeling right now," and gently bring your attention back to the present.

Mindfulness Practice:

The Five Senses Grounding Technique

This is a simple way to center yourself when your mind feels scattered or overwhelmed. It uses your senses to bring you back to the present moment.

Take a Deep Breath: Start by inhaling deeply through your nose and exhaling slowly through your mouth. Let your body relax.

Focus on Your Surroundings: Look around and name 5 things you can see.

Identify 4 things you can feel (like your clothes, the chair, or the ground).

Listen for 3 things you can hear (birds, a clock ticking, distant voices).

Notice 2 things you can smell (or imagine a favorite scent).

Take a sip of water or think of 1 thing you can taste.

Breathe Again: Take another deep breath, feeling more grounded and present.

This technique is especially helpful during moments of stress or anxiety, giving your mind a chance to slow down and regroup.

Everyday Mindfulness

You don't need to set aside hours to practice mindfulness, it can become a natural part of your day.

Here are some ways to incorporate it into your routine:

Mindful Eating: Pay attention to the colors, textures, and flavors of your food. Chew slowly and enjoy each bite.

Mindful Walking: Notice the feeling of your feet on the ground, the rhythm of your steps, and the sounds around you.

Mindful Breathing: Take a few deep breaths whenever you feel stressed or distracted. Focus only on the rise and fall of your chest.

Mindfulness and Emotions

One of the hardest parts of mindfulness is sitting with uncomfortable emotions without trying to push them away.

But here's the secret: when you allow yourself to fully feel an emotion, whether it's sadness, anger, or fear, it often passes more quickly than if you resist it.

Try this the next time you're upset:

Close your eyes and take a deep breath.

Name the emotion you're feeling:

"I feel angry," or "I feel nervous."

Notice where you feel it in your body, maybe it's a tight chest, a sinking stomach, or a heavy heart.

Breathe into that sensation, allowing it to be there without judgment.

As you breathe, remind yourself: "This feeling is temporary. It will pass."

Learning to sit with and accept uncomfortable feelings takes practice, kindness and patience with yourself.

It is helpful to understand that when we resist or judge a feeling, it tends to intensify; whereas when we allow and accept what is occurring, this creates space for it to move and change into a new experience.

Becoming Present in the Moment

Mindfulness isn't about controlling life's storms, it's about learning to stand in the rain, fully present, until the clouds part.

With practice, you'll find that even the toughest days can hold moments of peace and clarity.

Keep showing up for yourself, one mindful moment at a time.

Reflection Questions:

What's one small moment today where I can pause and practice mindfulness?

How does my body feel when I take a few deep breaths? What's one thing I noticed today that I often overlook?

Affirmations for Mindfulness:

"In this moment, I am whole. I don't need to fix anything or change anything, I am enough, just as I am."

"In this moment, I am here, I am grounded, I am enough."

Chapter 5: The Universal Connection: You Are Part of Something Bigger

♥

On tough days, it can feel like you're all alone, like no one understands what you're going through. But the truth is, you are part of something vast, something beautiful, and something bigger than yourself. The world is full of people, animals, plants, and nature, all of us interconnected, like pieces of a great cosmic puzzle. When you take a step back and look at the bigger picture, it's easier to see that your struggles, though hard, are part of the larger flow of life. Life isn't always easy, but it is always moving forward, like a river carrying everything in its path, and you are part of that journey.

Visualization: Your Cosmic Connection

Close your eyes and imagine yourself standing under a vast sky. See the stars twinkling above, the earth beneath your feet, and the trees reaching toward the heavens. Imagine yourself as part of this great universe, your heartbeat syncing with the rhythm of the earth. Know that just as the sun rises every day, so do you. You are part of a cycle of growth, change, and renewal.

Affirmation for Universal Love:

"I am connected to all of life. The universe holds me, loves me, and supports me. I am part of something much bigger than myself."

The Universal Connection: You Are Part of Something Bigger

Seeing Yourself as Part of the Whole Sometimes it's hard to believe you belong when you feel small or unsure of yourself. But think of the universe as a giant puzzle: every piece is unique and essential, including you. Without you, the puzzle would be incomplete. Here's how you can start seeing yourself as part of the whole:

1. Recognize Your Impact Every action you take, big or small, creates a ripple. When you smile at someone, help a friend, or care for the environment, you're making a difference. The kindness you share can inspire others and contribute to the world in ways you may not even see. Take a moment to reflect: What's one kind thing you've done

recently? How might it have affected someone else? Even if it feels small, it matters.

2. Connect with Nature Spending time in nature is one of the best ways to feel connected to the universe. Go for a walk, sit under a tree, or watch the sunset. Notice how the earth provides for you, the air you breathe, the ground beneath your feet, the beauty all around you. As you observe nature, you'l begin to see that you're part of the same rhythm and flow. Just as a tree grows toward the sun and rivers carve through mountains, you're growing and evolving, too.

3. Practice Gratitude for the Bigger Picture Gratitude helps you see the beauty in your connection to the world. Start by listing three things you're grateful for each day, whether it's the warmth of the sun, a good conversation, or even your favorite song. When you practice gratitude regularly, it becomes easier to notice how the universe supports you, even on hard days.

4. Embrace Your Unique Role

You are here for a reason. Maybe you don't know what that is yet, and that's okay. Your purpose doesn't have to be something grand, it could be as simple as being kind to others, expressing your creativity, or growing into the best version of yourself. Trust that your journey is unfolding exactly as it's meant to, and that the universe is holding space for you as you discover your path.

What Does it Mean to Be Connected?

Have you ever looked up at the stars and felt a sense of awe, as if you were part of something so much bigger than yourself? Or maybe you've stood in nature, surrounded by trees, the sound of the wind, and the warmth of the sun, and felt a deep sense of calm and belonging.

That feeling is your connection to the universe. It's the reminder that you're not alone, that you're part of an intricate, beautiful web of life that includes people, animals, plants, and the earth itself.

When life feels overwhelming, it's easy to forget this connection. You might feel isolated, like no one understands what you're going through. But the truth is, we're all connected. Every experience you have, every emotion you feel, is part of a larger flow of life. When you take a step back and see the bigger picture, it becomes easier to face your challenges with strength and hope.

Why is This Connection Important?

Feeling connected to the universe can: Provide Comfort in Tough Times: Knowing you're part of something bigger helps you realize that your struggles, while hard, are not permanent or insurmountable. Remind You of Your Worth: You matter. Just as every star contributes to the brilliance of the night sky, your existence adds value to the world. Inspire Resilience: Like rivers that carve through rock and trees that grow through cracks in the pavement, you have the strength to persevere, no matter what obstacles you face.

Seeing Yourself as Part of the Whole

Sometimes it's hard to believe you belong when you feel small or unsure of yourself. But think of the universe as a giant puzzle: every piece is unique and essential, including you. Without you, the puzzle would be incomplete.

Visualization: The Universe Embrace

The Universe Embrace is a visualization exercise designed to help you feel connected to something greater than yourself, offering comfort and reassurance during tough times. It's about recognizing that you are part of a vast, beautiful universe that holds you, supports you, and reminds you that you are never alone.

How to Practice the Universe Embrace

1. Find a Quiet Space.

Choose a place where you feel safe and relaxed. It can be your room, a cozy corner, or even outside in nature. Sit or lie down comfortably. You can close your eyes if it helps you focus.

2. Take a Few Deep Breaths

Inhale deeply through your nose for 4 seconds, allowing your belly to expand. Hold the breath for 4 seconds. Exhale slowly through your mouth for 6 seconds, releasing tension with each breath. Repeat this cycle a few times until you feel calm and centered.

3. Begin the Visualization

Imagine yourself standing under a vast night sky, filled with stars. The air is cool and gentle, and the earth beneath your feet feels solid and supportive. As you look up, notice the stars twinkling, like a million tiny lights connecting everything in the universe. Picture yourself as part of this great expanse. Feel how the stars, the earth, and the sky are all connected, just as you are connected to the world around you.

4. Feel the Universe's Support

Visualize a warm, golden light radiating from the center of the universe, surrounding you like a gentle embrace. This light represents love, compassion, and connection. Let it wrap around you, filling you with warmth and reassurance. Imagine the light flowing into your heart, syncing with your heartbeat and reminding you that you are part of something much bigger than yourself.

5. Reflect on Your Place in the Universe

As you stand in this light, think about the ways you are connected to others, friends, family, nature, and even people you've never met.

Remind yourself:

"I am part of the same energy that moves the stars and the oceans."

"I belong here. The universe holds me with love and support."

6. Close with Gratitude Before opening your eyes, take a moment to thank yourself for practicing this exercise. Express gratitude for the universe and the connections it provides, no matter how small or big.

Optional Additions to Enhance Practice

Journaling: After the visualization, write down how you felt. Did you notice a sense of calm or connection? What did the golden light symbolize for you?

Affirmations:

Repeat affirmations during or after the exercise, such as:

"I am never alone; I am connected to the universe."

"I trust the flow of life and my place in it."

Pairing with Nature:

If possible, practice this exercise outside under the stars, near a body of water, or in a park. Being in nature can deepen your sense of connection.

When to Use This Exercise

When you feel lonely or disconnected. During moments of stress or overwhelm. As part of a nightly ritual to unwind and feel grounded before bed.

Connecting Thought

The Universe Embrace reminds you that no matter how isolated you may feel, you are part of something vast, loving, and interconnected. Each time you practice this exercise, you strengthen your connection to the world around you and to your own heart. The universe holds you, and you belong.

Teachings on Awakening, Guidance, & Living in Harmony

When you tune into the deep silence within, you connect to the light of your soul and receive messages from divine intelligence. A new path of opportunities and challenges awaits, but to embrace it, you must let go of the past, old burdens, beliefs, and limiting habits. In moments of stillness, you may sense guidance from the higher realms. This guidance offers a gift from the universe: peace and harmony within. Peace is a compass for the soul, and when you feel it in your heart, it signifies alignment with your higher self.

The Era of Transformation

The current time is one of increasing awareness within humanity, marking a transition into an era of transformation. To align with these higher possibilities, it's vital to meditate, connect to the energy of the Earth, and raise your vibration. Practices like deep breathing and meditation help you attune to the rhythm of the universe, bringing peace and guidance from higher consciousness.

The Power of Silence

Silence is not emptiness but a bridge to divine wisdom. In the stillness, answers arise, and the language of the soul becomes clear. Use your words as spiritual seeds, focusing on love, truth, and light. Affirmations such as "I am the embodiment of peace and light" protect your energy field and reinforce positivity.

Nurturing Your Energy Field

Protect your energy by visualizing a bright light surrounding you, maintaining a calm mind, and purifying your environment. Connect with nature and live fully in the present, as time is a temporary experiential reality. Every moment offers a lesson, and living in the now opens the door to expanded awareness. Love as the Answer Love is the most powerful energy in the universe. It transcends emotion, heals wounds, and inspires others. Choose love over fear in every moment. Love not only transforms your life but also becomes a beacon for those around you.

Prosperity and Creativity

True prosperity stems from an abundant mind and soul, not material possessions. Embrace creative energy, explore new skills, and turn every moment into an opportunity to create and share abundance. Small acts of kindness ripple outward, inviting more prosperity into your life.

Forgiveness and Letting Go

Forgiveness is a gift to yourself, freeing your heart from past wounds. Letting go of resentment liberates you to move forward in lightness and peace. Old habits and limiting beliefs are burdens that can be released through reflection and mindful change.

The Practice of Meditation

Meditation is a tool for connecting with divine intelligence and breaking free from the illusions of the limiting beliefs and identities of the past. In stillness, you observe thoughts and emotions without attachment, realizing your true nature as the infinite light within. Spend time each day in meditation, allowing divine energy to guide you.

Living with Divine Awareness

Life is not random; every moment is an opportunity to give love and serve as a channel for divine energy. Even small actions, when performed with love and dedication, contribute to universal harmony. Each person is a ray of light capable of transforming darkness.

Embracing Challenges and Growth

Difficulties are opportunities to grow and reveal your inner light. By trusting the flow of life and aligning with divine intelligence, you overcome fear and resistance, finding strength in your journey.

The Essence of Awakening

Awakening begins by looking inward and realizing the core essence of your heart. The light of your soul, free from the past, shines brightly, guiding you and inspiring others. Each step forward is a chance to be reborn, leaving behind the past and embracing the infinite potential of your higher self. You are a beautiful being of love and a radiant heart, a torchbearer in the world.

Trust the light within and allow it to guide you through all challenges. Live in love, awareness, and harmony, knowing that you are never alone. Every breath, every step is a prayer and a connection to the universe. Let your presence illuminate the path for yourself and others.

Chapter 6:
Self-Confidence:
Trusting Yourself

♥

Remember, confidence isn't about never falling; it's about knowing you'll always rise. You might not always feel confident, especially when your body and emotions feel out of balance. But true confidence doesn't come from feeling perfect; it comes from trusting yourself, no matter what you're going through. When you trust yourself, you trust your ability to weather any storm, to face challenges, and to keep growing. You know that even on the toughest days, you will rise again, stronger and wiser.

What is Self-Confidence?

Self-confidence is the belief in your ability to handle challenges, make decisions, and navigate life's ups and downs. It's not about being perfect or never making mistakes, it's about trusting yourself to keep going, even when things get tough. Confidence doesn't always mean feeling bold or fearless. Sometimes, it's quiet and steady, like a small flame that reminds you, "I can do this." Even on days when you feel uncertain, building self-confidence is about showing up for yourself, one step at a time.

Why is Self-Confidence Important? Self-confidence helps you: Take on New Challenges: When you trust yourself, you're more likely to step out of your comfort zone and try new things. Bounce Back from Setbacks: Confidence reminds you that failure isn't the end, it's part of learning and growing. Feel Empowered: Instead of looking for validation from others, self-confidence comes from within, giving you a sense of independence and strength. Treat Yourself with Compassion: Confidence isn't about perfection; it's about accepting yourself as you are, flaws and all.

What Holds Us Back from Confidence?

It's normal to have moments of self-doubt, especially when life is full of uncertainty. Here are some common challenges: Comparing Yourself to Others Social media, friends, and even family can make you feel like you're not good enough. But remember: everyone's journey is different. Just because someone looks confident on the outside doesn't mean they don't have their own struggles.

Fear of Failure: Failing doesn't mean you're not good enough, it means you're trying, learning, and growing. Confidence is built by embracing mistakes and using them to improve.

Negative Self-Talk: The way you talk to yourself matters. If you constantly tell yourself, "I can't do this" or "I'm not good enough," it can chip away at your confidence.

How to Build Self-Confidence

Celebrate Small Wins: Confidence doesn't come from one big moment, it's built through small victories. Did you try something new, even if it felt scary? Celebrate that. Did you stand up for yourself or complete a challenging task? Acknowledge your effort.

Focus on Your Strengths: Everyone has unique skills and qualities that make them special. Take a moment to write down three things you're good at or proud of. These strengths are part of what makes you, you.

Practice Positive Self-Talk: When self-doubt creeps in, counter it with positive affirmations. For example: Instead of: "I'm going to mess this up."   Try: "I'm doing my best, and that's enough." Instead of: "I'm not as good as them." Try: "I have my own strengths, and I bring something unique to the table."

Take Action: Confidence grows when you prove to yourself that you can handle challenges. Start with small steps, like speaking up in class or trying a new hobby. Each time you face a fear, you'll feel a little stronger.

Surround Yourself with Supportive People: Spend time with people who lift you up, encourage you, and believe in your abilities. Avoid those who bring you down or make you doubt yourself.

Self-Confidence Affirmation Practice: Every morning, stand tall and say to yourself, " I trust myself. I have the strength to handle whatever comes my way. I am learning, I am growing, and I am capable."

Self-Confidence Practices:

The Power Pose: Your body language can affect how you feel. When you need a confidence boost, try the Power Pose: Stand tall with your feet shoulder-width apart. Place your hands on your hips or raise them high above your head, like a superhero. Hold this pose for 1-2 minutes while taking deep breaths. This posture sends signals to your brain that you're strong and capable, helping you feel more confident instantly.

Affirmation for Self-Confidence: "I trust myself. I have the strength to handle whatever comes my way. Each day, I grow more confident in who I am and what I can do."

Reflection Questions: What's one thing I've done recently that I'm proud of? How can I remind myself of my strengths when I'm feeling unsure? What's one small step I can take today to step outside my comfort zone?

In Summary

Self-confidence is about believing in your ability to grow, adapt, and rise, no matter the challenges you face. It isn't about being fearless. It's a skill you can nurture over time, and every time you choose to trust yourself, you're building a stronger foundation for the future.

Keep practicing, and remember: you are capable, you are worthy, and you've got this.

Chapter 7: Emotional Self-Awareness: Understanding Your Inner World

♥

E motional self-awareness is the ability to recognize and understand your emotions, what you're feeling, why you're feeling it, and how it's affecting your thoughts and actions. Think of it as being able to "read" your own emotional weather forecast. Are you feeling sunny and calm? Or are there storm clouds gathering? Being aware of your emotions doesn't mean you have to control or fix them. Instead, it's about noticing them without judgment and using that awareness to make thoughtful decisions.

Why is Emotional Self-Awareness Helpful?

The more aware we are of our feelings, sensations and emotions, the more options we have for how to respond to ourselves and any given situation. It is useful to have more information when making decisions and navigating life's uncertain waters. Being more emotionally aware means you can observe your feelings without necessarily needing to react or express them, but simply be aware of how you feel to give more meaning to your experience.

When you understand your emotions, you can:

Make Better Decisions: Emotional self-awareness helps you pause and respond thoughtfully, rather than reacting impulsively. For example, if you're feeling angry, you can recognize it and choose to cool down before saying something hurtful.

Build Stronger Relationships: When you know how you're feeling, you can communicate it to others in a healthy way. This builds trust and understanding in your relationships.

Reduce Stress and Overwhelm: Naming and understanding your emotions can help them feel less intense. Instead of being consumed by a feeling, you can step back and observe it.

Develop Self-Compassion: When you're aware of your emotions, you're more likely to treat yourself with kindness. You can recognize when you're struggling and give yourself the care you need.

Boost Your Confidence: Understanding your emotions helps you feel more in control of your inner world, which builds self-trust and confidence.

Principles of Emotional Self-Awareness

Emotions Are Signals

Emotions aren't random, they're signals from your body and mind, telling you what you need. For example, anger might signal that your boundaries are being crossed, sadness might mean you need rest or comfort, and anxiety might be a sign to prepare for something important. By understanding these signals, you can begin to see emotions as valuable guides rather than obstacles.

Emotions Are Temporary

No feeling lasts forever. Emotions, like waves, rise and fall. When you become aware of your feelings, you can ride them out without getting stuck in them. Knowing that emotions are temporary can help you find the strength to endure challenging moments, trusting that they will pass.

You Are Not Your Emotions

Your emotions don't define you, they're just part of your experience. You can feel angry without being an "angry person," or feel sad without being a "sad person." Recognizing this separation can help you approach emotions with curiosity rather than judgment.

Awareness is the First Step

You can't manage or respond to emotions you're not aware of. That's why paying attention to what you're feeling is so important. Developing emotional awareness creates the foundation for managing your emotions effectively.

How to Practice Emotional Self-Awareness:

Name Your Emotions

When you feel something strong, pause and ask yourself: "What am I feeling right now?" "Where do I feel this in my body?" Be as specific as possible. For example, instead of saying "I feel bad," try "I feel disappointed" or "I feel frustrated." Naming your emotions helps you understand them better.

Track Your Emotional Patterns

Keep a journal to record your emotions each day. Note what triggered the feeling, how it affected you, and how you responded. Over time, you'll notice patterns that can help you better understand yourself and predict how you might feel in similar situations.

Pause Before Reacting

When an emotion feels intense, take a moment before responding. Try the "Stop, Breathe, Reflect" method: Stop: Pause for a moment. Breathe: Take a few deep breaths to calm your body. Reflect: Ask yourself, "What am I feeling, and how do I want to respond?" This pause allows you to act thoughtfully rather than impulsively.

Check-in With Yourself

Throughout the day, take a few moments to ask, "How am I feeling right now?" This helps you stay connected to your emotions and prevents them from building up unnoticed. Regular check-ins foster emotional awareness and balance.

Practice Mindful Observation

When you notice an emotion, imagine yourself as a scientist observing it with curiosity. For example: "I feel nervous. My heart is racing, and my palms are sweaty. This usually happens before I speak in class." This practice helps you separate yourself from the emotion, so you can observe it without judgment and respond effectively.

Day-to-Day Applications

Before a big decision check in with yourself: Are you feeling calm and clear-headed, or are emotions clouding your judgment? Give yourself time to process your emotions before making a choice.

When You're Upset

Instead of reacting immediately, name the emotion and pause. For example, "I'm feeling really angry right now because I felt ignored." This approach helps you respond thoughtfully instead of lashing out.

In Conversations

If you're feeling overwhelmed during a conversation, say, "I need a moment to process what I'm feeling." This can prevent miscommunication and give you time to respond with clarity and care.

At the End of the Day

Reflect on your emotions from the day. Ask yourself: "What emotions did I feel today?", "What triggered those emotions?", and "How did I handle them, and what could I do differently next time?". Taking time to reflect helps you learn from your experiences and approach future emotional challenges with greater confidence and resilience.

Relationships and Conflict Resolution

Conflict is an inevitable part of life, emerging from our interactions and differences. While it might seem daunting, conflict is not inherently negative. Often, it signals an opportunity for understanding, growth, and improved relationships. When handled constructively, disagreements allow us to explore diverse perspectives and uncover hidden truths. They challenge us to communicate better, listen more intently, and consider alternate viewpoints. Conflict becomes a catalyst for growth when approached with an open mind, ready to learn and adapt. This perspective transforms discord into a valuable experience, fostering personal development and strengthening the bonds we share with others.

Effective conflict resolution requires strategies that promote collaboration and mutual understanding. Collaborative problem-solving emphasizes the importance of working together to find a solution that satisfies everyone involved. By encouraging open dialogue and creative thinking, this approach allows participants to express their needs and concerns freely. Focusing on common goals rather than individual positions fosters a spirit of cooperation and teamwork. Similarly, win-win negotiation addresses the underlying interests of all parties, aiming to satisfy everyone involved. This technique requires empathy and flexibility, as understanding others' motivations and desires is key to finding solutions. By prioritizing these skills, you can transform conflicts into opportunities for connection and growth.

Resolved conflicts often lead to stronger, more resilient relationships. Approaching disagreements constructively deepens understanding and trust. Imagine two colleagues clashing over a project deadline. By openly discussing their concerns and working together to find a mutually beneficial solution, they not only resolve the conflict but also build a stronger partnership. This process fosters respect and appreciation for each other's strengths and perspectives, enhancing their ability to collaborate in the future. In personal relationships, navigating disagreements with patience and empathy cultivates deeper connections. Each resolved conflict becomes a testament to the relationship's resilience, demonstrating that differences can coexist with harmony and respect.

Preventing future conflicts involves setting clear intentions and mutually agreed upon expectations. By establishing guidelines for behavior and communication, misunderstandings can be minimized, reducing the likelihood of disagreements. Regular relationship check-ins provide an opportunity to address concerns or adjust expectations proactively. These conversations foster transparency and trust, ensuring that everyone's needs are acknowledged and respected. Maintaining open lines of communication strengthens the foundation of a relationship, making it more adaptable and capable of weathering future challenges.

Conflict resolution is not about eliminating disagreements but transforming them into opportunities for growth. By embracing conflict as a natural part of relationships, you can navigate disagreements with confidence and compassion. This approach fosters understanding and connection, turning potential obstacles into stepping stones for personal and relational development. Cultivating these skills leads to more resilient and fulfilling relationships, capable of supporting you through life's inevitable ups and downs.

Integrating Your New Awareness

Developing emotional awareness can be achieved through various exercises that help identify, understand, and process emotions. Start with an emotion check-in, pausing throughout the day to ask yourself what you're feeling, where you feel it in your body, and what might be causing it. Pair this with a body scan to deepen physical awareness by noticing sensations like tension or tightness and reflecting on the emotions they might represent. Journaling is another powerful tool, write about recent emotional experiences, noting the triggers, your responses, and what you'd do differently next time.

Creative exercises, such as emotion sculpting, allow you to visually explore emotions through drawing or painting, while the "name it to tame it" technique involves labeling your emotions to reduce their intensity. Use a mood map to track patterns over time, noting triggers, intensity, and frequency of emotions. For a step-by-step approach, practice the Emotional ABCs: acknowledge the feeling, breathe deeply to calm yourself, and choose how to respond.

Empathy exercises help you understand others' emotions by considering their perspectives, while role-playing scenarios can enhance your ability to recognize and manage emotional triggers. Finally, balance your emotional awareness by reflecting on positive experiences through gratitude and joy exercises, identifying three moments each day that brought happiness or appreciation. These practices, when done consistently, can cultivate a deeper connection to your emotions and improve emotional resilience.

Chapter 8: The Invitation to Keep Growing

♥

Your journey is about growth, learning, and finding your own path. And it's okay not to have all the answers right now. Life isn't about having everything figured out, especially when you're young or starting a new life.

Each day is a new opportunity to become a little more of who you are meant to be. The more you practice self-compassion, mindfulness, and connecting to the larger world, the more you'll see that everything, even the hard days, are part of your beautiful unfolding story.

When facing challenges it is helpful to remember that each day is an opportunity to be the hero in your own epic story. We can choose to develop new skills, keep an open mind, learn to be compassionate and interested in finding new approaches. Maintaining an attitude of curiosity will lead you to develop a growth mindset, always searching for understanding and further adventures on your path.

There is a basic tenet of recovery that says focus on honesty, open mindedness and willingness to find new solutions and explore different perspectives. This world is a great arena for experimenting with new ideas, solutions and problem solving innovations. You have something unique and meaningful to contribute, lets discover what your gifts and abilities are all about!

In a world that seems to constantly evolve beneath our feet, it's natural to feel a profound sense of uncertainty. Life brings about varied seasons of change, each carrying potential triggers for anxiety, stress, and worry. It's my genuine hope that through this book, you'll discover a sanctuary of support, understanding, and practical tools to navigate your life's journey.

We all strive to forge paths brimming with fulfillment, connection, meaning, and purpose. However, when faced with change, loss, crisis, or unexpected challenges, our foundational sense of security may feel deeply threatened. It's crucial, then, to have previously established a framework of self-support, compassion, and practical skills to help us traverse life's turbulent moments.

The Connection Between Acceptance and Change

The journey of life is one of continual growth, discovery, and transformation. To be human is to be ever-changing, learning from each experience, and expanding into new versions of ourselves. This invitation to keep growing is not about rejecting who we are in this moment; rather, it is about embracing both self-acceptance and the potential for change. The balance between these two truths, loving ourselves as we are and striving to become more, lies at the heart of emotional maturity and personal fulfillment.

Growth is a natural and necessary part of life. Just as plants stretch toward the sun and rivers carve new paths, we too are designed to evolve. When we stop growing, we risk stagnation and the loss of opportunities to explore the richness of life. Learning new skills, seeking out new perspectives, and challenging ourselves to step beyond our comfort zones all contribute to a deeper sense of purpose and meaning. Growth keeps us engaged with the world, curious about its mysteries, and open to its possibilities.

At the same time, true growth is rooted in self-acceptance. To grow authentically, we must first recognize and honor who we are in this moment. This means cultivating compassion for our strengths and our struggles, our triumphs and our failures. It means acknowledging that we are worthy and whole, even as we strive to become more. Without this foundation of self-love, the pursuit of growth can feel like an endless quest for perfection, leaving us disconnected from the present and from ourselves.

The dialectic between self-acceptance and change invites us to hold space for both gratitude and aspiration. It encourages us to appreciate the journey we have traveled so far while remaining excited about the path ahead. This balance allows us to approach growth not as a form of self-criticism, but as an act of self-celebration. Each step forward becomes a testament to our resilience, courage, and capacity for renewal.

Heartfulness plays a central role in this process. When we approach ourselves with a mindful heart, we create a safe and nurturing environment for growth. Heartfulness reminds us to be gentle with ourselves, to honor the pace of our journey, and to celebrate even the smallest victories. It also encourages us to extend this same compassion to others, recognizing that growth is a shared experience. By supporting one another in our individual and collective transformations, we build a community that thrives on connection and mutual respect.

The decision to keep growing also requires a willingness to embrace uncertainty. Growth often involves venturing into the unknown, taking risks, and facing challenges that test our limits. It is in these moments of discomfort that we discover our true strength and resilience. Each challenge becomes an opportunity to learn more about ourselves and the world around us. With heartfulness as our guide, we can face these moments with courage and trust, knowing that they are an integral part of our evolution.

Affirmation:
"I am enough just as I am. Every day, I grow stronger, wiser, and more connected to my own heart and to the world around me."

Chapter 9: The Hero's Journey: Becoming the Hero of Your Own Epic Story

♥

E very single one of us is living a story. Some days, it feels like a grand adventure, a story brimming with possibility, love, and connection. Other days, it feels like a tragic tale, full of heartbreak, loss, or failure.

But what if I told you that your story, all of it, every messy, complicated, beautiful piece, is part of a much larger narrative? What if, like the myths and legends passed down through generations, you are the hero of your own epic journey?

Joseph Campbell, in his groundbreaking work The Hero with a Thousand Faces, reveals a pattern that he called the "monomyth" or the "hero's journey." It's a universal story structure found in myths across cultures and times, a cycle of separation, initiation, and return. Campbell's work teaches us that the hero's journey isn't just for gods and legends; it's for you and me.

We are all heroes, navigating our own journeys to seek redemption, forgiveness, purpose, or some transcendent truth. And the beautiful thing?

This journey is sacred, even when it doesn't feel that way. So, let's break it down. Let's walk together through the stages of the hero's journey and see how each of us, in our own messy, human way, is called to something greater.

The Call to Adventure

The hero's journey begins with a call to adventure, often sparked by discomfort, dissatisfaction, or an undeniable longing for something more. In myths, this might be a magical summons or a fateful encounter. In our lives, it might look like a job loss, the end of a relationship, a diagnosis, or even a quiet yearning in the middle of an ordinary day. The call is rarely convenient or expected. It interrupts our comfort and asks us to step into the unknown.

Think about a moment in your life when you felt an ache for something greater, a purpose, a change, or a truth you couldn't ignore. Maybe it was deciding to leave a toxic job, go back to school, or end a relationship that no longer served you. Those moments are invitations. They're the universe whispering, "It's time."

For me, one of my calls to adventure came in the form of vulnerability. As someone who had spent years armoring up and avoiding emotional risks, the call was terrifying. But it came in whispers I couldn't ignore:

"You can't truly connect with others unless you let them see you."

I resisted, of course, most heroes do. But deep down, I knew that answering the call was the only way forward.

The Refusal of the Call

Here's the thing about the call to adventure: it's scary. It asks us to leave behind what we know and venture into the unknown. And so, like any reasonable person, we resist. We say, "I'm not ready." We cling to the safety of the familiar, even when it's no longer serving us.

This is the stage where fear shows up, often disguised as practicality or self-doubt. How many times have you felt the pull to change but talked yourself out of it? "It's not the right time." "I'm not good enough." "What if I fail?" The refusal of the call is part of the process. It's a natural response to fear, and it's okay.

But here's what Campbell teaches us: the call will keep coming. It might change form or grow louder, but it will not disappear. And eventually, something will push us forward.

Crossing the Threshold

At some point, we step over the threshold. Maybe it's by choice, or maybe life pushes us. Either way, we leave the known world and enter the unknown. This is the beginning of transformation.

In myths, this might be the moment the hero leaves their village or sets sail. In our lives, it's the moment we say, "Yes," even if our voice shakes. Crossing the threshold often comes with a mix of fear and exhilaration. It's the decision to start therapy, move to a new city, or have a difficult conversation.

For me, it was the moment I committed to studying vulnerability. It felt like stepping into the dark, unsure of what I might find. But it was also freeing, because it meant I was moving.

The Trials and Tests

Here's the hard truth: the hero's journey is not a straight path. Once we step into the unknown, we face trials and tests that challenge us to grow. In myths, these are dragons to slay or riddles to solve. In life, they're the setbacks, failures, and heartbreaks that test our resolve. These moments can feel overwhelming. They can make us question why we ever left the comfort of the familiar. But they are essential. It's through the trials that we develop resilience, courage, and self-awareness.

Think about a time in your life when you faced a significant challenge. Maybe it was navigating a loss or overcoming self-doubt. Now think about who you became because of that experience. The trials shape us in ways we often can't see until later.

The Revelation and Transformation

Every hero's journey leads to a moment of revelation, a discovery of truth, purpose, or strength that changes everything. This is the heart of the journey. It's the moment the hero realizes they have what they need to overcome their challenges.

It's Luke Skywalker trusting the Force or Frodo accepting his role as the ring-bearer. For us, it might be the moment we realize that forgiveness is not for others but for ourselves, or that our worth isn't tied to our achievements. Revelation often comes after struggle.

For me, it was the realization that vulnerability isn't weakness, it's courage. That shift changed everything. It didn't erase my fear, but it gave me the strength to keep going.

The Return

The final stage of the journey is the return. The hero comes back to their world, changed by their experiences, and ready to share their wisdom. This is the moment of integration, bringing what we've learned back into our lives and using it to make a difference. It's not about perfection; it's about authenticity and service.

For us, the return might look like using our pain to help others, speaking our truth, or simply living more fully and intentionally. It's realizing that the journey isn't just about us; it's about how we show up in the world.

Your Divine Quest

Here's the thing: we are all on a divine quest. Each of us is here to learn, grow, and contribute something only we can offer. Whether it's seeking redemption, forgiveness, or a transcendent goal, the journey is uniquely ours. And just like the heroes of myth, we are not alone. Along the way, we'll find allies, mentors, and guides who remind us of our strength and purpose.

Maybe your quest is to heal from a painful past, find your voice, or create something meaningful. Maybe it's to love deeply, forgive fully, or simply live with more presence and joy. Whatever it is, know this:

your journey matters. You matter. And even on the hardest days, you are a hero in the making.

So, my friend, what is your call to adventure? What truth or longing is whispering to you, asking you to step into the unknown? The journey won't be easy, it never is. But it will be worth it. Because at the end of the day, the hero's journey is not about reaching some distant destination. It's about becoming. It's about stepping into your story with courage and saying, "This is who I am. This is why I'm here."

The Beginning of Your Story

This isn't the end of the book, it's the beginning of a new chapter in your life. You now have tools to help you navigate tough days and find balance, but the story you're writing is entirely your own. Take it one moment, one breath, one wave at a time. Be patient with yourself. Celebrate your progress, no matter how small. And always remember: you are enough, just as you are.

Conclusion: The Journey Continues

❤

No matter where you are in your journey, remember that every feeling, every challenge, and every moment is part of the story of you. And no matter how difficult things may seem right now, you have the tools, the strength, and the love to move through it. Take it one breath at a time. Be gentle with yourself. And know that no matter what, you are never alone.

Life is full of waves, some are gentle ripples, others are fierce storms. But every wave you ride teaches you something new about yourself and the world around you. The journey of self-discovery, resilience, and growth isn't about avoiding the waves; it's about learning how to navigate them with courage, compassion, and trust in yourself.

The Power of Your Toolkit

Throughout this book, you've gathered tools to help you through life's tough days:

Understanding the Storms

Recognizing that your feelings, while intense, are temporary and part of being human.

Self-Compassion: Learning to be your own best friend and treating yourself with kindness.

Breathing Through the Waves: Using the power of your breath to find calm in the chaos.

Mindfulness: Staying present in the moment, even when it's hard.

Universal Connection: Remembering that you're part of something bigger and that you belong.

Self-Confidence: Trusting your ability to face life's challenges and grow stronger with each experience.

These tools are here for you whenever you need them. They're not about fixing you, you're not broken. They're about helping you tap into the strength, love, and potential that already exist within you.

In an ever-evolving world, where change is the only constant, it's entirely natural to experience a profound sense of uncertainty. Our lives are marked by distinct seasons of change, each laden with its own set of challenges that can trigger feelings of anxiety, stress, and worry.

My deepest hope is that this book becomes a beacon of support, offering you understanding, and arming you with practical tools to navigate the complex journey of life.

We all yearn to carve out lives filled with fulfillment, deep connections, meaningful experiences, and a strong sense of purpose. Yet, the inevitable encounters with change, loss, crisis, or unforeseen challenges can shake our foundational sense of security to its core.

In these moments, the importance of having a well-established personal framework, comprising self-support, compassion, and a set of practical skills, becomes undeniably crucial. This framework acts as our anchor, enabling us to navigate through life's tumultuous waters with grace and resilience.

Embracing the Uncertainty

Life doesn't come with a map, and that's okay. It's full of twists, turns, and surprises. Some days will be easier than others, but each one is an opportunity to learn, grow, and move forward. Even when things feel uncertain, trust that you are capable of navigating the unknown.

Every step you take, no matter how small, is part of your unique journey. And while you might not have all the answers right now, you're learning, adapting, and becoming more of who you're meant to be.

You Are Always Connected

On those days when life feels overwhelming, remember this: you are never truly alone. The universe is vast, but it's also deeply connected. The same energy that moves the stars and the oceans flows through you. There are people who care about you, friends, family, teachers, and even strangers who may cross your path at just the right time. And there's always a space of stillness and support within yourself, waiting for you to return to it.

Final Affirmation:

"I am resilient, I am worthy, and I am growing every day. Life's waves may challenge me, but they will never break me. I trust myself, and I trust my journey."

As you close this book, carry these words with you: You are strong. You are loved. You are part of something bigger. This is just the beginning, and the universe is cheering you on. Keep riding the waves, and know that you have everything you need to find your balance, your peace, and your power.

The End (Or Rather, a New Beginning)

References

Baer, R. A. (2015). Mindfulness and self-compassion: A clinician's guide. Guilford Press.

Brown, B. (2010). The gifts of imperfection: Let go of who you think you're supposed to be and embrace who you are. Hazelden Publishing.

Chodron, P. (2012). Taking the leap: Freeing ourselves from old habits and fears. Shambhala Publications.

Kabat-Zinn, J. (2013). Full catastrophe living: Using the wisdom of your body and mind to face stress, pain, and illness (2nd ed.). Bantam Books. Linehan, M. M. (2015). DBT skills training manual (2nd ed.). Guilford Press. Neff, K. D. (2011). Self-compassion: The proven power of being kind to yourself. HarperCollins.

Nhat Hanh, T. (2015). The miracle of mindfulness: An introduction to the practice of meditation (Rev. ed.). Beacon Press.

Siegel, D. J., & Bryson, T. P. (2011). The whole-brain child: 12 revolutionary strategies to nurture your child's developing mind. Delacorte Press.

Thich Nhat Hanh. (2011). Peace is every step: The path of mindfulness in everyday life. Bantam.

Williams, M., Teasdale, J., Segal, Z., & Kabat-Zinn, J. (2007). The mindful way through depression: Freeing yourself from chronic unhappiness. Guilford Press.

Campbell, J. (2008). The hero with a thousand faces (3rd ed.). New World Library. (Original work published 1949)

Wikipedia contributors. (n.d.). Sati (Buddhism). In Wikipedia. https://en.wikipedia.org/wiki/Sati_(Buddhism) Tricycle. (n.d.). The meaning of sati. https://tricycle.org/magazine/sati-meaning/ Dunne, J. D. (n.d.). On the translation of sati. In Tricycle. https://en.wikipedia.org/wiki/Sati_(Buddhism)

Make a Difference

♥

U nlock the Power of Generosity "The best way to find yourself is to lose yourself in the service of others." – Mahatma Gandhi If this book has helped you in any way, would you take a moment to share your thoughts?

Kindness has a way of making ripples. Even the smallest act, like leaving a simple review, can help someone else find exactly what they need at just the right moment. Would you help someone just like you, someone looking for ways to feel more calm, confident, and resilient, but unsure where to start?

My mission is to make inner strength and emotional well-being simple, approachable, and real. This book was written to be a guiding light for anyone navigating stress, self-doubt, or life's unexpected storms. But to reach more people who need it, I need your help.

Most people choose books based on reviews. That means your words could be the reason someone else finds the tools and encouragement they've been looking for. A review takes less than a minute, but it could make all the difference for someone feeling lost or overwhelmed.

Your review could help...One more person find a sense of peace on a tough day. One more reader feel seen, understood, and supported. One more heart believe in their own resilience. One more mind embrace confidence and calm.

If this book has helped you in any way, would you take a moment to share your thoughts?

Your kindness and generosity mean more than words can express. Thank you from the bottom of my heart for being a part of this journey! H. M. Mann

About The Author
H. M. Mann

H. M. Mann is a mental health professional with 27 plus years of experience providing support, insight and guidance to people of all ages and backgrounds. Offering an eclectic therapeutic approach based on the needs of the individual, H.M. Mann specializes in working with those who identify as sensitive or emotionally empathic. Please follow future publications within the Inner Radiance Series.

www.ingramcontent.com/pod-product-compliance
Lightning Source LLC
La Vergne TN
LVHW051815080426
835513LV00017B/1966